BEING CATHOLIC IN A CHANGING WORLD

Jeffrey LaBelle, SJ,
and Daniel Kendall, SJ

PAULIST PRESS
New York/Mahwah, NJ

Cover design by Joy Taylor
Book design by Lynn Else

Library of Congress Cataloging-in-Publication Data

LaBelle, Jeffrey.
    Being Catholic in a changing world / Jeffrey LaBelle and Daniel Kendall.
        p. cm.
    Includes bibliographical references (p.   ).
    ISBN 978-0-8091-4611-6 (alk. paper)
    1. Christian life—Catholic authors. 2. Catholic Church. I. Kendall, Daniel. II. Title.
    BX2350.3.L33 2009
    282—dc22
                                                                2009025624

Published by Paulist Press
997 Macarthur Boulevard
Mahwah, New Jersey 07430

www.paulistpress.com

Printed and bound in the
United States of America

CONTENTS

v

*To Robert and Josephine LaBelle
in gratitude for the gifts of life, love, and faith*

*To Anne Kendell
and Richard and Judy Inderrieden
for their love and friendship over the years*

INTRODUCTION

During the almost half-century that has passed since the Second Vatican Council (1962–65), the world has not remained static but has been constantly changing. Today people wonder about the future of the Catholic Church in such areas as organization (especially the papacy), morality, and technology in a post–9/11 world. "Is it possible," they frequently ask, "to disagree with official Church teaching and still remain a 'good Catholic'?" Organized lay ministry and service in the Vatican pattern is something relatively new; meanwhile, "immersion programs," voluntarism among college students, and "service programs" among those of high school age have also influenced the local Church. After the Council of Trent (1545–63), Catholics had often left reading the Bible to Protestants, were officially forbidden to share in non-Catholic religious services, and frequently doubted the possibility of non-Catholics being saved. So, many Catholics after Vatican II were surprised to find their leaders encouraging them to engage in dialogue with other Christians and with non-Christians. Pope John Paul II even accepted an invitation in 1985 to address 100,000 young Muslims in Morocco. People wanted to know: "Just what is our relationship to non-Catholics (and non-Christians)?" Most recently, cyberspace has made an impact on all of us, as well as fear of terrorism and xenophobia (fear of foreigners) in the post–9/11 world.

These are issues that we will consider in this book. In the early twenty-first century, what can the Church offer people who have questions about these areas? We plan to take a historical (rather than a doctrinal) approach that shows us where we have been and indicates paths to follow that are in continuity with our rich past. Some of today's problems are quite obvious. Factionalism in political life spills over into the Church. Recently the Pew Landscape Survey (2008) notes that "while nearly one-in-three Americans (31%) were raised in the Catholic faith, today fewer than one-in-four (24%) describe themselves as Catholic." The report continues: "These losses would have been even more pronounced were it not for the offsetting impact of immigration. The Landscape Survey finds that among the foreign-born adult population, Catholics outnumber Protestants by nearly a two-to-one margin (46% Catholic vs. 24% Protestant); among native-born Americans, on the other hand, Protestants outnumber Catholics by an even larger margin (55% Protestant vs. 21% Catholic). Immigrants are also disproportionately represented among several world religions in the U.S., including Islam, Hinduism and Buddhism."[1] Since, according to the Landscape Survey, in recent years 7 percent of United States citizens who were raised as Catholics do not practice their faith, there is no reason to think that this trend will not continue after today's immigrants blend into the mainstream.

As Catholics, what can and should we do? In his opening speech to the bishops gathered for Vatican II, Pope John XXIII mentioned that history is the teacher of life.[2] We will follow the pope's advice, and recall our collective history in areas of crucial concerns to renew and strengthen a Church that will be relevant for future generations. Students of history realize that Pope John's call for adapting the Church to the modern world was not all that new, but rather it was something that the Church has done periodically since the time of Jesus Christ. Though the Bible itself has strong Semitic overtones, early Christians looked to people like Clement of Alexandria, Origen, Basil, Jerome, and Augustine in the second, third, fourth, and fifth centuries to translate Jesus' message into Greco-Roman terms. Later on, in the twelfth and thirteenth centuries, Bernard, Thomas Aquinas, Bonaventure, and Duns Scotus adapted Jesus' teaching to the medieval world, using new insights gained from experience. But early in the twentieth century, most of the theological insights taught in Catholic schools in the United States were still shaped by the teachings of the Council of Trent (1545–63). That particular Council was convoked to answer questions posed by the Protestant Reformation. The world changed radically during the next four hundred years. Since the sixteenth century, the theories of Galileo, Newton, and Kepler challenged traditionally held views in the area of science; Descartes and Kant offered philosophies that focused on the subject rather than the object; Darwin's theory of evolution shook the world; and the implementation of Karl Marx's theories affected the daily lives of millions of people. Could and would the Church say something positive about the contemporary world rather than condemning it? With new questions and problems that had arisen by the 1960s, people hoped that the Church might say something more relevant to the modern world than merely repeat the decrees of the Council of Trent. Vatican II was given the task of providing the Church with an "updating" (*aggiornamento*, as Pope John XXIII called it) for the twentieth century. Since Vatican II, the computer has come of age, wars in Vietnam and Iraq have polarized people, and the sexual revolution has challenged long-established moral values. New dilemmas have accompanied advances in technology. How does the Church confront the twenty-first century?

We are especially grateful to our mutual friends Richard and Judy Inderrieden for urging us to write this book. Like many people today, they want to know how Catholics, members of an old organization, can apply their faith to a rapidly changing situation. Chris Bellitto, academic editor at large for Paulist Press, encouraged us to use a "case approach." He pointed out that readers can resonate with real, concrete examples, even if the examples we give are generally composites based on experience, with substitute names. Not only do examples focus the question, but they give the readers an opportunity to consider similar situations in their own lives. That is what we have tried to do. We are most grateful to Chris for his suggestions and the great help that he has given us in writing this book. Father Gerald O'Collins, SJ, has generously advised us on the issues that we discuss in this book. We appreciate his support and generosity.

Jeffrey LaBelle, SJ, and Daniel Kendall, SJ
July 31, 2008

NOTES

1. Pew Landscape Survey, http://pewresearch.org/pubs/743/united-states-religion.
2. "Opening Speech to the Council," in W. M. Abbott and J. Gallagher, *The Documents of Vatican II* (New York: America Press, 1966), 712.

CHAPTER ONE

CHURCH ORGANIZATION AND THE PAPACY

Since the beginning of the third millennium many lay groups have arisen such as Voice of the Faithful. Although these groups have no official standing, they make their views heard on contemporary issues. Church leaders cannot ignore them. How have bishops, especially those in the United States, reacted? Let us look at a typical situation that exists in Catholic higher education.

CASE

Rebecca has a doctorate in theology earned at a Catholic university. She has been teaching in a Catholic university in the United States for over twenty years. In the early 1990s she and her colleagues had heard about a directive from the pope that spoke of higher education. Its name was *Ex Corde Ecclesiae* ("From the heart of the Church"). The document talked about the relationships between Catholic theological faculties and the local bishop. After reading it, Rebecca and her colleagues decided that the document was aimed mainly at European universities where, frequently enough, the State provided the salaries for theology professors. The State usually asked the local bishop before making appointments, so that leaders of the official Church would approve new professors as representing the Church. In a real sense, the bishop was acting as an agent who mediated between the Church and the State.

Such was not the case in the United States where Catholic colleges and universities are private but subject to accrediting agencies if they are to be credible institutions. If the official Church were to have veto power over an appointment, or a bishop could force the institution to dismiss a person who had already begun teaching, then that institution would not only lose its credibility, but it usually could also be sued by the professor in question. The bishops could also see problems in implementing such a document in the United States.

The United States Conference of Catholic Bishops (USCCB)* studied this document until 1996 and, looking at the role of the Catholic university, urged "mutual trust" and "continuing dialogue" between the bishops and the colleges and universities, but did nothing else. When officials in Rome received this news, they asked the United States bishops to go back to the drawing board. The bishops did, and came up with another, preliminary document in 1999. Finally, in 2000, the bishops completed their work.

According to the bishops, beginning in 2001, all Catholics teaching theology in a Catholic college or university were told to request a *mandatum* from the local bishop. A *mandatum* is a document stating that the teacher is committed to teaching "authentic Catholic doctrine." This is something that a bishop could withdraw at any time by saying that what a professor taught was not in keeping with what the bishop judged to be Catholic teaching (whether that be true, or whether there were many diverse opinions on a given issue). Obviously, if a person

---

*The USCCB is the official organization of the Catholic hierarchy in the United States. It is a canonical entity governing the Church and its public policy arm.

did not seek nor have a *mandatum*, then a bishop could not withdraw it. There was no way bishops could enforce this in the case of laypersons. The administration of institutes of higher learning could bring pressure to bear on a professor to seek a mandatum, but few cared or wanted to do so. The bishops went on to say that the majority of the boards of trustees and the majority of professors teaching theology should be Catholics.[1]

When Rebecca asked her fellow theology professors in 2001 what they planned to do, most said that they did not intend to seek the *mandatum*. One reason they gave for this stance was that the local bishop did not have an advanced degree in theology. Who was he to judge people who knew more about their area of expertise than he did? The university president supported them. When the local bishop asked the president for a list of the Catholics who were teaching theology, the president said that, because of the privacy laws in his state, he could not give the bishop a list of who were and who were not Catholics. Since the *mandatum* was supposed to be a matter between the individual and the local bishop, the president later stated that he could not ask individuals if they had or had not requested the *mandatum*. The president added that whether a person had requested the *mandatum* was not an issue that could be raised when a person was being considered for promotion and tenure.

The local bishop then checked the university catalogue for the names of the people in the department, and subsequently wrote to all faculty members—Catholic, Protestant, Jewish, and Muslim—strongly suggesting that they seek the *mandatum*. Of course, the latter three groups did not fall under the local bishop's authority.

The result was that none of the faculty applied for the *mandatum*. By having one, they had nothing to gain and much to lose.

COMMENT

These "norms" were too much for most Catholic universities to accept. In the case just mentioned, the bishop's request for information on teachers' religious affiliations was not appropriate in civil law. This real example indicates that, even today, those who are in positions of power and authority in the Church, from the pope on down, worry about differing points of view and want to impose their own outlooks in a juridical way.

Today, we might also ask: What is the role of authority? Does it consist in power? Or can authority exist as a witness to some religious belief or moral way of acting? Does the Catholic Church operate in a manner that Jesus expected? Did Jesus leave his followers an organizational blueprint? Or did the current operating model develop in response to various needs over the centuries, and change as new circumstances and problems arose?

HISTORICAL BACKGROUND

When we begin with Scripture we see that the Gospels really give us almost no clue as to what Jesus' thoughts were on the matter. The closest passage that might give us some insight occurs in Matthew 16:18–19, where Jesus is quoted as saying (NRSV translation): "And I tell you, you are Peter, and on this rock I will build my church, and the gates of Hades will not prevail against it. I will give you the keys of the kingdom of heaven, and whatever you bind on earth will be bound in heaven, and whatever you loose on earth will be loosed in heaven." Problems with this passage include the use and understanding of the word *church*.

4

Church in the Old Testament (Hebrew: *qahal*) simply means the "people of God." In the passage just cited, we ask ourselves: "Was Jesus speaking only to Peter, or also to Peter's successors? Was Peter's leadership to be one of being an example of faith, or was it one of juridical authority in the Church?" These issues are not clear, especially when we look at Peter's role in the rest of the New Testament.

The word *church* occurs frequently in the letters of St. Paul. His writings are the earliest documents in the New Testament because his active life as a Christian began five or six years after Jesus died. Paul used the term *church* to describe local congregations (for example, the church at Corinth, the church at Rome). In his early epistles he does not tell us how the congregations were organized. Rather, he spoke of the theological meaning of "church," whose members are "the body of Christ," with Christ as the head. Scholars dispute the Pauline authorship of the Pastoral Epistles (1 Timothy, 2 Timothy, Titus). In any case, however, they form part of the New Testament. We see in them a primitive structure of early Church leadership. These three epistles speak of bishops, deacons, and elders (sometimes translated as "priests"). Bishops seem to be the leaders of the community, although there is no clear talk of an organized clergy. Deacons were those designated to take care of the community's finances (Acts 6:1–7). Apostles formed a unique group in the New Testament, and were chosen specifically by Jesus; so nowhere do we find the apostles appointing people to succeed themselves precisely as apostles.

Peter does not seem to have played a large role in the organization of the local churches. For instance, James was head of the church in Jerusalem (James 1:1), and Paul organized many churches in what is now Turkey and

Greece. Peter's function seems to have been mainly that of being a witness. Though we read of Peter bringing converts to Christianity, we do not have any records of his establishing a local church.

By the beginning of the second century, St. Ignatius of Antioch (c. 35–110) spoke of the Church being where the local bishop was (*Letter to the Smyrnaeans* 8). The local bishop's job was to guard the Church against heresy. Ignatius wrote letters still extant when he was on his journey to death as a martyr in Rome. Despite persecutions such as the one Ignatius experienced, the Church continued to grow.

During the reign of Constantine (c. 312–37) Christianity went from being persecuted to become the official state religion. Instead of meeting in people's homes, early Christians were able to designate and construct buildings specifically for worship. A professional group of people called "clergy" came into being to lead worship in the communities. The early Church was not without its theological problems, however. Various issues beset the Church as a whole, so councils were called to make decisions regarding doctrine. Those who attended these councils were mainly bishops. Bishops of the more populated regions began to take more prominent leadership positions. When the Roman Empire in the West came to an end in the fifth century, the most prominent post in the Church was that of the Bishop of Rome. By that time influential cities that had large Christian populations included Alexandria, Antioch, Constantinople, and, of course, Rome. As various empires came into being and others went out of existence, the Church with its hierarchical leadership continued.

In the year 1054, the Churches in the eastern part of the old Roman Empire split from the western part, although the formal break was centuries in the making. These Churches called themselves "Orthodox." They retained the structure of a hierarchy, but had no single head such as the pope. Thus, they rejected the idea that the pope, the Bishop of Rome, had juridical control over them. Although the pope might be the "successor of Peter," the Orthodox did not accept that he was equal to the apostle Peter. Their other beliefs differed very little from those of the West. In the West, people still looked to Rome for leadership. One structural difference that would take place in the Roman Church was the imposition of celibacy on the clergy by the First Lateran Council (1123), whereas the Orthodox allowed a married priesthood. Both groups had monks who observed celibacy.

Over the centuries, various communities have split off from both these groups. The most radical split was that of the Reformation in the sixteenth century. It affected the Roman Church more than the Orthodox Churches. One notable group that retained much of the Roman Catholic beliefs and structures were the Anglicans. However, they too did not accept the decisions of the Bishop of Rome as authoritative. Most of the reformers, however, challenged not only some of the teachings, but also the very structure of the hierarchy.

Because Jesus was *the* high priest of the New Covenant (Heb 9:11), the reformers replaced priests with ministers. Since the reformers recognized only baptism and the Lord's Supper as sacraments, becoming a minister was not necessarily a lifelong commitment nor considered a sacrament. The emphasis in worship was more on the preaching of the Word, rather than on the Roman practice of elaborate ceremonies. Local congregations soon controlled the various church communities. The minister did not always have the final voice in decisions and was often selected by the community. Thus, the minister needed to please the community. Both the reformers and the Roman Church realized the need for an educated clergy, and so set up seminary systems. Given this state of affairs, the Roman Church convoked the Council of Trent (1545–63) to decide its stance on both its own structure and doctrine. From an organizational point of view, Trent reaffirmed its hierarchical view of the Church (with its centralization in Rome). After all, the enemies were many, and a strong defense against their ideas was needed. Both sides uncompromisingly held to their structural and theological positions.

As the centuries after Trent passed, the popes sought less and less input from laypeople and priests as to who should be selected for the positions that opened up in various dioceses. Although bishops were seen as the local heads of the Church, the First Vatican Council (1870) decreed that the pope had jurisdiction in each individual diocese. With that came more uniformity and more control by the pope over local affairs.

At the time of the First Vatican Council, the Church in the United States was growing rapidly. Bishops needed money to erect more churches and schools. To obtain loans from the banks, each diocese was incorporated as a "Corporation Sole." That means that, with few exceptions such as hospitals and colleges that belonged to religious congregations and orders, the local bishop had title to or controlled just about everything in his diocese. All the buildings and real estate could be used for collateral when the diocese needed to borrow money. Not only did the local parishes give the diocese a certain percentage of money received in donations, but they were often required to take up special collections for the diocese. In most cases the people who gave the money were not consulted on the way the money was to be used.

The twentieth century began with tight control from Rome over local bishops, and the bishops over the priests. Laypeople were left completely out of the administrative picture. All this had effects on the intellectual life. If those who had powerful positions in the Vatican bureaucracy did not want something taught, written, or published, they could force their will on local bishops and religious superiors. Since most of the teachers in Catholic elementary schools were nuns, while priests, brothers, as well as nuns staffed Catholic high schools, control was fairly complete. Tenure came to Catholic colleges and universities rather late in the twentieth century. As a result, teachers in higher education watched what they said and taught if they wanted to retain their jobs. To be a Catholic meant to have one's life regulated in its spiritual, intellectual, and moral spheres by celibates who were educated in a certain mentality. That mentality was dogmatic in outlook.

CONTEMPORARY SCENE

Where is the Church today? Over the last half-century many factors, usually isolated, have converged to force changes. As the population of the United States grew, more and more people matriculated in public universities and were exposed to pluralistic viewpoints. People's friends and spouses did not necessarily belong to the same faith. After 1970, the number of priests, nuns, and brothers decreased dramatically in the schools because of the lack of vocations. More and more laypeople filled the gap by earning degrees in theology and religious education, and took the place of priests and religious in classrooms. Younger people, especially, were skeptical about authority. Simultaneously, the teachings of the Second Vatican Council supported change. The Church promoted ecumenism, defined itself as "the people of God" (not "the Church and the [lay] people"), and has tried to be more historical in its outlook.

Soon after Vatican II ended, "parish councils" were established. Although advisory, those who served as members were usually elected by the parish itself and not appointed by the pastor. Both men and women participated. The next step was to initiate a "financial council" in the parishes. Pastors realized that they were not always experts on investments, fundraising, and similar activities. Why not use the brains of the parish? After all, the parish belonged to the parishioners as much as it did to the pastor. Not all of this happened without opposition. Yet Vatican II's call for more involvement on the part of the whole community had its good effects.

At the beginning of the twenty-first century, Catholics were shocked by the news of sex scandals among the clergy. They discovered that a few presumably celibate priests—some very highly respected men—had been preying on their sons and daughters. Their shock was compounded by the fact that some of their bishops knew much about this bad conduct but did little or nothing to correct it. People sued and forced bishops to take action. Dioceses gave large amounts of money to victims and their families. Some dioceses were forced to declare bankruptcy. Because of the financial burdens caused by the lawsuits, several dioceses decided to move away from the "Corporation Sole" model, and to incorporate each parish separately. That way they hoped to avoid future bankruptcy. Since laypeople would be on the boards of these new corporations, they would have an active voice on how the money would be spent and would gain some local control over the parish.

From the above examples, we see that changing mentalities comes with difficulty. In the case of the Catholic Church, we are talking about millennia, not just centuries. In parallel cases, when we examine, for instance, the practice of political democracy over the course of time, we see its advances and setbacks. Not everyone in the world today thinks that democracy is a good thing. In a worldwide organization like the Church, which includes so many different cultures, change is even more complex than it is in democracies. People at all levels need to see the value of such change. Even if people agree that change is necessary, they do not always agree on the form that the change should take.

Hopefully, in the Church, we are dealing with people of good will. Many bishops have initiated "listening sessions" to find out what people's concerns are. Some even value people's "solutions." The sharp decline in priestly and religious vocations has already changed the demographics of the Church. Laypeople have a better understanding of theology today than in past centuries. Some also occupy key positions on university faculties and publish their views. A few have been appointed chancellors of their diocese. Even today we witness the reaction of people when some Church leaders "condemn" or give "warnings" about certain books or movies. The books sell better and the movies frequently become hits. As a result of Vatican II, the Church abolished the "Index of Forbidden Books." Although it had existed for centuries, it was not too effective. Even before the Index was abolished, many people no longer believed that their eternal salvation depended on whether they read or did not read a certain book.

The expansion of knowledge will force Church leaders more and more to use cogent arguments rather than authoritative power, if they want to convince people of their viewpoints. The challenge to the Church today is to communicate the Gospel in a credible manner. As people become better educated, any "authoritarian model" of the Church will suffer less and less credibility.

QUESTIONS FOR DISCUSSION

1. Does my parish (or diocese) promote adult religious education? Why, or why not?
2. If my parish or diocese promotes religious education, how qualified are the teachers? How much "freedom of expression" do they allow in discussions?[2]
3. In my parish or diocese, how wide is the consultation process with regard to issues such as spending money, promoting social justice issues, and making parish life more than passive attendance at Sunday Mass?
4. Is any type of evaluation process in place that looks at areas such as quality of liturgies (and homilies) in parishes, the effectiveness of outreach programs, the involvement of people in the parish in making decisions, and so on?
5. Does my parish or diocese use a collaborative model or a hierarchical model in its day-to-day functions?

SUGGESTED READINGS

Today any discussion on the material covered in this chapter should begin with reading the documents of the Second Vatican Council. Especially pertinent are the documents on the Church (*Lumen Gentium*), revelation (*Dei Verbum*), liturgy (*Sacrosanctum Concilium*), the Church today (*Gaudium et Spes*), the laity (*Apostolicam Actuositatem*), and education (*Gravissimum Educationis*). The United States Conference of Catholic Bishops (USCCB) maintains a Web site (http://www.usccb.org/) that contains official statements of both the Vatican and the United States bishops on the various issues mentioned in this chapter, in addition to other subjects such as marriage, family life, violence, and so on. Authors like Gerald O'Collins and Richard McBrien have written extensively on issues facing today's Church. A glance at the various books published by Paulist Press will give an overview of contemporary and diverse viewpoints on most of the topics covered in this chapter.

NOTES

1. "Article 4," *Ex Corde Ecclesiae* (http://www.usccb.org/education/excorde.htm).

2. People unqualified in theology frequently consider themselves "experts" in interpreting official statements of the Church. Consider this message before the 2008 elections in the United States to the people of the Diocese of Tucson from its bishop, Gerald Kicanas: "I emphasize again to our parishes the importance of following the 'Political Activity Guidelines for Catholic Organizations' from the Office of the General Counsel of the U.S. Conference of Catholic Bishops (www.usccb.org/ogc/guidelines.shtml). It has been our experience that some well-meaning parishioners will approach their parishes with requests to 'educate' their fellow parishioners about the stands that candidates take on various issues and about the various ballot initiatives.…Also, in regard to the various 'Catholic' voting guides that appear during election campaigns, in our Diocese the only approved voter information materials that

can be provided to parishioners at our parishes are 'Forming Consciences for Faithful Citizenship' from the USCCB, resources of the Faithful Citizenship Program (www.faith fulcitizenship.org)" (August 11, 2008, http://www.diocese tucson.org/mondaymemo.pdf).

CHAPTER TWO

FACTIONALISM WITHIN THE CHURCH

CASE

Mike and Janet are parents of children who are in grammar school. Mike is a doctor. He has volunteered to serve on his parish's school board and to coach Little League. Recently their new pastor, relatively young (thirty-six years old), decided that the school was entirely his responsibility. He fired the nun who was a very effective principal because he believed that she should wear a traditional religious habit. He then changed the school's daily schedule to require all students to attend daily Mass. Obviously making the children come to school half an hour earlier worked a hardship on the parents. He also wanted his associate pastor to teach the "religion classes." His next move was to change the school's curriculum since he thought that the current one was too "Lutheran."

Mike soon realized that the pastor really did not want a school board. What bothered him the most, however, was that the quality of his children's education was declining, and that what passed as religious instruction was somewhat dated. He wondered if the high tuition he and Janet were paying was misspent. They consulted two of their priest friends who were teaching theology at the college level. The priest-professors agreed: the quality of theological instruction was inferior.

Although Mike and Janet were faced with a painful decision, they decided to take their children out of school. They were lucky that they lived in an urban area where other good schools, both public and private, were available. The added burden, however, was that the other schools involved a longer drive for them each day. Obviously their support of the parish soon ended.

COMMENT

This story exemplifies a number of issues. What stands out most glaringly is that the pastor, who was not a professional educator, was trying to force his will on people who knew more about grammar school education than he did. He did not even ask the school board about his decisions. He also wanted students to learn a regressive theology. The parents, on the other hand, well educated and intelligent, took their responsibility toward their children seriously. Initially they were willing to accept the pastor's imposition of an early daily schedule even if it involved some hardship, but when they realized that, in the larger picture, it meant their children would be receiving an inferior education in several areas, they chose the path that would help their children. They also discovered that there was no way they could talk to or negotiate with the pastor.

HISTORICAL BACKGROUND

Similar situations have been with the Church since its very first days. The earliest accounts are found in the letters of St. Paul. Beginning with his first missionary journey, St. Paul proclaimed that a new era had begun with Jesus' life, death, and resurrection. He told Gentile converts that the Mosaic Law, with its demands of circumcision for men and dietary norms for men and women, did not bind them. Yet some people in the community demanded that the male converts be circumcised and tried to force everyone to observe the dietary laws. One can imagine the tension between the two groups. Like the example cited above, some people tried to impose an old theology on people.

St. Paul himself became quite angry when he saw this situation. He wrote the Galatians that he was surprised some of them were "turning to a different gospel—not that there is another gospel, but there are some who are confusing you and want to pervert the gospel of Christ" (1:6–7). He went on to condemn their attitude by saying, "We know that a person is justified not by the works of the law [circumcision, dietary prohibitions] but through faith in Jesus Christ" (2:16). He later repeated his same premise that "neither circumcision nor uncircumcision counts for anything; the only thing that counts is faith working through love" (5:6). He concluded by telling those who forced Gentile converts to keep the Mosaic Law that they had missed the whole point of his message. "For neither circumcision nor uncircumcision is anything; but a new creation is everything!" (6:15).

Although Christianity began in Palestine in a Semitic environment, it moved rather quickly to Rome. To make their message credible, the early missionaries needed to explain Christianity's teaching in the main language of the Roman Empire. At that time the main language was Greek, at least in educated and business circles. Putting these new ideas into Greek involved more than making translations; it involved using Greek categories and concepts. Hebrew (as well as the local language that Jesus spoke, Aramaic) was rather simple compared to the nuanced Greek. Greek lent itself to making distinctions and offering new insights.

At the end of the first century, people asked questions such as: Was Jesus only divine? Was Jesus only human? These questions later developed into speculation about the number of wills and minds Jesus had. Did Jesus have more than one intellect—a divine one or a human one? Could Mary be called the "Mother of God" or only "Mother of the Human Jesus"? Questions like these divided early Christian communities during the first five centuries of the Christian era. There were factions on both sides. Yet such discussions promoted the intellectual life of the Church. Debates on these topics enlivened people. Church councils were convened to discuss these issues and attempted to find formulations of Christian belief that were satisfactory to most people and in line with New Testament teaching. Still, factions of this type continued for more than five hundred years and some people were sent into exile because of their views.

Sometimes divisions were not universal but regional. For instance, in the eighth century, some Christians in the eastern part of the old Roman Empire worried about having pictures or icons in their churches and using them in religious services. They thought this was idolatry and began a campaign to smash them. Though the controversy was rather localized and lasted a relatively short time, it was revived again in the sixteenth and seventeenth centuries by some leaders of the Reformation.

Although divisions occurred on religious issues, differences were also political and cultural. As a result, in 1054, the Orthodox East split from the Latin West over the role of the papacy and the manner in which doctrine was to be interpreted. That separation was so deep that it remains today, although the formal acts of excommunication were mutually lifted in 1965. Even though various attempts have been made to heal the divisions, so far they have failed. It is amazing how two Churches can still be so similar, yet after 1,000 years have not been able to reconcile their differences.

After the split between the East and the West, various medieval groups arose such as the Albigensians (those that held a dualistic theology with Satan being equivalent of a god), and people like John Hus and John Wycliffe, who fought for the Bible being read in people's own language and also spoke against the "crimes" of the Roman Church. The most widespread aspects of factionalism were yet to come. Martin Luther (1483–1546) is the best known among all those connected with the Protestant Reformation. Luther was a Scripture scholar and his translation of the Bible into German helped to form that language. The spark that ignited Luther's pent-up emotions was the rebuilding of St. Peter's Basilica in Rome. To obtain funds for this massive undertaking, the Church sent a Dominican, Johann Tetzel, to preach on "indulgences." For donating a certain amount of money, people could receive an indulgence to have their sins forgiven as well as God's punishment due to those sins removed. Luther responded that God alone could forgive sins. The Church was acting like the Pharisees whom St. Paul had opposed. They were the people who thought that works rather than faith in God would bring forgiveness. In addition to disagreeing with this practice, Luther listed another ninety-four reasons (theses) and, in 1517 supposedly nailed them on a church door. For all practical purposes, this marked the beginning of the Reformation. Factionalism became the order of the day.

Luther's life and the beginning of the Reformation coincided with the discovery of the New World. Colonization and the imposition of the Christian faith on the conquered people was common. The split between the Roman Church and the Protestant religions became wider and wider. Persecutions arose in Europe over religious differences that were deep and strong. Because of this situation, many people immigrated to North America so that they could practice their beliefs according to their consciences. When these immigrants eventually founded the United States, they set up a democratic form of government (a rather novel idea at the time) that tolerated all religions. Not uncommonly did family members have different faiths, and, frequently enough, even a husband and wife may have belonged to different Christian denominations.

During the last two hundred years, three events have significantly impacted the various factions within Christianity: Vatican Council I (1870), the formation of the World Council of Churches (1948), and Vatican Council II (1962–65). Vatican Council I reaffirmed the strong role of the pope, something which alienated rather than helped the factions come together. The World Council of Churches set as its goal discovering ways of achieving some type of unity among Christians. Although Vatican II was internal to the Catholic Church, it reached out to other faiths and invited people of other religious beliefs to attend its deliberations.

CONTEMPORARY SCENE

What has been the main stumbling block that has formed and retained barriers against Christians coming together? The example we cited at the beginning of this chapter gives us an indication. What most people find offensive today is the way power is exercised, especially in the hierarchical Church. People resent arbitrary decisions being made with no input from those who are supporting the structure, especially financially. These decisions can involve some day-to-day issues (such as tuition-paying parents wanting more of a voice in the direction that their children's school follows), as well as other concerns such as clerical celibacy or the ordination of women and married men.

Any organization as old as the Catholic Church naturally has inertia in making change. Since over one billion people belong to the Church, there is quite a variety of opinions on any serious question or issue. Some people believe that, even if a situation might be bad, any change would make it worse. Their solution is to do nothing. Others believe that they can prevent change or force certain changes by giving or not giving financial support. Still others believe that bad publicity will force Church leaders to change.

Since Pope John XXIII committed the Church to a historical approach to her mission, we might look at the options that such a perspective offers. We must also consider other factors involved in today's world, especially the increased awareness of the interdependence that people have on each other. Men and women are more open to other viewpoints as they visit and live in foreign countries, marry into different cultures, and have better educations. They might look into the historical reasons why certain practices exist, and then question whether these reasons still bind us today. The first Christians did this in the earliest days of the Church, when they decided not to impose the Jewish dietary laws on converts, and moved the day of worship from Saturday to Sunday. In doing this they were making decisions about practices found in the Hebrew Scriptures with a view to making it relevant to the new Gentile members. There is a precedent for making such changes.

When we look at the split of Christianity in 1054, the Reformation in the sixteenth century, and finally, the problems of today, one theme keeps recurring over the last millennium: the role of authority, particularly as found in the papacy. What is the papacy's function? Over the centuries the Church and the papacy have evolved from being something both spiritual and temporal to that of being only spiritual. At the same time, as it has become more spiritual, it also has become more centralized. That centralization has affected both its organization and thought. A certain uniformity has emerged. Might that be counterproductive?

At the beginning of this chapter we spoke of the pastor who used his position to assert his will on the grammar school. He did not have many restraints put on him to prevent him from doing as he pleased. As one moves up higher in the hierarchy, fewer and fewer people are in a position to curb that person's authority. Let us take an example:

CASE

Mary has her doctoral degree in business. She is an associate professor at a leading university in her state. Since she is interested in learning more about her religion, Mary also obtained a master's degree in theology from a Catholic university. Recently she substituted for a sick teacher at a catechism class in her parish on a Sunday morning. To make the children feel comfortable with her, a stranger, she thought she would begin with an easy question: "How many sacraments are there?" One girl put up her hand and said: "For men there are seven; for women there are six. Women cannot be ordained." That was not an answer that Mary expected. She thought for a moment, and then realized this little girl had articulated a very thorny point that had many levels of meaning.

Mary decided to investigate why this was so, because she

knew other denominations had women priests and even bishops. Why should the Catholic Church be so different? On what grounds was this difference based? After all, most Christians in the twenty-first century agree on the Scriptures.

In Mary's research she found out that, in 1994, Pope John Paul II had said: "I declare that the Church has no authority whatsoever to confer priestly ordination on women and that this judgment is to be definitively held by all the Church's faithful."[1] She wondered: "Why is there no debate on the subject? Are Catholics the only persons enlightened enough on this issue to know the truth?" She realized that, at least on the official level, with one directive the pope had tried to shut off all discussion of the matter. Did people accept his judgment?

Obviously many women did not believe that the debate was over. In 2002, seven women were ordained in a ceremony on a boat on the Danube River. They were excommunicated by Cardinal Ratzinger (now Pope Benedict XVI). In 2006, a similar ceremony took place near Pittsburgh. The Diocese of Pittsburgh responded with a statement that said "those who by their presence give witness and encouragement to this fundamental break with the unity of the People of God place themselves outside the Church."[2]

Mary wondered what harm could come from an open discussion of the subject. Did some leaders in the Catholic Church have a monopoly on intelligence?

CONTEMPORARY SCENE

This case study includes some current reactions to the Church's "official position" on the ordination of women. But are there other views we should consider? Cardinal Avery Dulles has written *Models of the Church*, in which he listed five models: institution, mystical communion, sacrament, herald, and servant.[3] Each one of these has good points and some drawbacks. For instance, as an institution, the Church can offer a leadership structure and a manifestation of unity. Yet, negatively, it can become rigid, doctrinaire, and conformist. If we consider the Church as "Sacrament," we see one of its attractive features is that it is a sign and instrument of grace to its members and to the world. On the other hand, it "could lead to a sterile aestheticism and to an almost narcissistic self-contemplation."[4] Dulles argues for a blend of the models (not that they are all equal in importance). Which model would Dulles rate as the least and most important? Dulles says:

> One of the five models, I believe, cannot properly be taken as primary—and this is the institutional model. Of their very nature, I believe, institutions are subordinate to persons, structures are subordinate to life....Without calling into question the value and importance of institutions, one may feel that this value does not properly appear unless it can be seen that the structure effectively helps to make the Church a community of grace, a sacrament of Christ, a herald of salvation, and a servant of mankind.[5]

If any model rises to the top in importance, Dulles would hold for the sacramental model.

> It preserves the value of the institutional elements because the official structures of the Church give it clear and visible outlines, so that it can be a vivid sign. It preserves the community value, for if the Church

were not a communion of love it could not be an authentic sign of Christ. It preserves the dimension of proclamation, because only by reliance on Christ and by bearing witness to him, whether the message is welcomed or rejected, can the Church effectively point to Christ as the bearer of God's redemptive grace. This model, finally, preserves the dimension of worldly service, because without this the Church would not be a sign of Christ the servant.[6]

Dulles added another model in a later edition of his book: discipleship.[7] He took it from Pope John Paul II's encyclical *Redemptor Hominis*. In the end, however, Dulles concludes that no single model addresses the fullness of God's call to the Church. Each model addresses a certain aspect. If we agree with Dulles's assessment, we note that the main problem people experience in today's Church is the overemphasis on the institutional model. Authority without the accompanying accountability rankles people the most. This can be seen in the example of the pastor as well as that of the pope.

QUESTIONS FOR DISCUSSION

1. How much authority should any consultative board (for example, a school board, a finance council) have in a parish or in a diocese?
2. How do we achieve some type of unity in diversity in a parish or diocese (that is, making allowances for opinions that are frequently at odds with each other)? How does a pastor or bishop include diverse elements when making decisions?
3. Should people openly discuss issues such as women's ordination, even though the pope has

made a definitive ruling, and asks that people no longer question the theological basis of his decision?

4. How can Church leadership de-emphasize an authoritative and institutional model, and move toward one that is more concerned about service than exists at the present time?

5. Over the centuries how has Church teaching changed on issues? Could it change on current issues? What are some of the presuppositions people have when they say that the Church can never change?

SUGGESTED READINGS

Both Dulles's book and Pope John Paul II's 1994 statement on the ordination of women (available at http://www.vatican.va/holy_father/john_paul_ii/apost_letters/documents/hf_jp-ii_apl_22051994_ordinatio-sacerdotalis_en.html) are primary sources for much of what we mentioned in this chapter. As mentioned in the last chapter, two documents from the Second Vatican Council directly touch upon the Church (*The Church* and *The Church in the Modern World*). Theologians such as Karl Rahner and Yves Congar have written extensively about the nature of the Church from a European perspective. Rosemary Chinnici, Francis Schüssler Fiorenza, John Fuellenbach, Ada María Isasi-Díaz, Elizabeth Johnson, Richard McBrien, and Gerald O'Collins are examples of contemporary authors who are actively writing in this area.

NOTES

1. *Ordinatio Sacerdotalis*, 4.

2. Diocese of Pittsburgh, news release, June 15, 2006.

3. Avery Cardinal Dulles, *Models of the Church* (Garden City, NY: Image Books, 1978).

4. Ibid., 195.

5. Ibid., 197–98.

6. Ibid.

7. *Models of the Church*, expanded ed. (Garden City, NY: Image Books, 1987), 207–10.

CHAPTER THREE

ACCEPTANCE OF DOCTRINE

How much of official doctrine must a person accept to be considered a Catholic? Is it possible to remain in the Church while disagreeing with some Vatican teaching? Is a person who denies the resurrection of Christ a Catholic? What about a person who differs from the Church's stance on same-sex marriages? How would we classify a person who thinks that the only "real" Mass is that which is celebrated in Latin? Why do we hear so much about these issues now? Are they all of the same importance? Obviously some of these areas are more essential to being a Catholic than others. This distinction has not always been carefully made.

Differences with "common teaching" are as old as the Scriptures. One need only look at the epistles of John to discover a movement among some in the early Church who did not believe that Jesus was really human. John even refers to such a person as being the anti-Christ (2 John 1:7). Members of the Church have debated similar questions of different significance over the centuries with varying reactions.

In the thirteenth century, the Inquisition was set up to root out heresy. During the following centuries, the Inquisition used torture to find out the "truth," and those who did not repent of their "errors" were severely punished. The Inquisition spread from Europe to the New World, where Spain and Portugal had colonies, as well as to India and the Philippines. Perhaps the most famous persons condemned by the Inquisition were Joan of Arc (who was put to death for having visions and hearing voices that were "false and diabolical") and Galileo (for holding that the sun and not the earth was the center of the universe; this was considered contrary to the literal meaning of Scripture). By the eighteenth century, the barbarous methods of the Inquisition had gradually faded out of the picture, though it remained a Roman office designed to protect the integrity of faith and condemn errors. However, the name (Congregation for the Universal Inquisition) lingered on until 1908, when it became the Congregation of the Holy Office. The new title changed little in the way it operated. Scholars like Pierre Teilhard de Chardin (1881–1955) were banned from publishing their findings. The Holy Office believed that Teilhard's writings were undermining the doctrine of original sin that had been developed by St. Augustine (354–430). Another change of name occurred in 1965 when it became known as the Congregation for the Doctrine of Faith, though its job description remained the same. Scholars like Jacques Dupuis (1923–2004) were warned for their views on religious pluralism (2000), and Jon Sobrino (1938–) for emphasizing the human nature of Jesus Christ, and downplaying his divine nature (2007). Perhaps the most famous person in charge of this office is Pope Benedict XVI. He was its "prefect" or leader from 1981 to 2005. Although this Roman office today is known for condemning theologians whose written views it disagrees with, these people are very few in comparison with the very many whose names are never mentioned.

Let us consider a typical case that we face on a daily basis. Though the following contemporary example is based on morality, its principles can be applied to other areas of theology.

CASE

Jim and Sue recently finished college. They met each other at work soon after graduation. The urban area in which they live is famous for its high rents. As young people just entering the workforce, they wished to have some money to spend besides paying rent and making car payments. They quickly realized that, if they shared an apartment and owned only one car, they would have money to spend on other things. As a result they moved into the same apartment and began living together. They may or may not get married. Before they even begin to think of marriage, they want to have some financial stability and a bit of "fun" in their lives.

Both Jim and Sue are Catholics and attended Catholic universities. They are usually present at Sunday Mass in their parish and receive communion. Some gay couples who are their friends help plan the music for the parish's Masses, and frequently go out with them to bistros on the weekends. None of them would miss receiving ashes on Ash Wednesday or palms on Palm Sunday. None of them sees any inconsistency between their lifestyles and being a Catholic in the twenty-first century. They are not arguing with anyone nor do they really care whether or not others agree or disagree with their views. All of them do volunteer work, especially helping to find shelter for the homeless. They take public transportation as much as possible to reduce emissions into the atmosphere, and realize that when they use too much paper, more trees will be cut down.

COMMENT

Several factors are at work here, not the least of which is the contemporary culture. Let us break this case study down into two areas: traditional moral theology and contemporary moral theology.

Traditional Catholic moral theology has based itself on a static and unchanging physicalist natural law approach. This means looking at human acts and judging their morality from a viewpoint as totally external or objective as possible. Factors in making such a judgment include examining what God has revealed, especially in the Bible, looking at past traditions, and reviewing the purpose of given human acts. This approach to the natural law tends to look at the human acts apart from any context. For instance, many people accept that the primary purpose of sexuality is to produce children. Any sexual act that does not lead to that is morally wrong. Obviously this must take place only within marriage. In making such a moral judgment, the context of the act is not always part of the consideration in the natural law approach. The result is that conclusions in Catholic moral theology have remained constant over the years regardless of time, place, and culture.

Since Vatican II, people have tended to take a wider view and ask themselves: "What does it mean to be a Christian at the present time and in the present circumstances?" Most are not concerned with limiting their reasoning to traditional natural law theories. They realize that many of its conclusions in the past have been tied to a time period, based upon limited knowledge, and have in mind circumstances that might no longer exist. Advances in thought need to be considered.

The Second Vatican Council spoke of the freedom of individuals to form their own individual consciences (see no. 16 of *The Church in the Modern World*—that is, *Gaudium et Spes*). Three years after the Council ended, Pope Paul VI issued his famous encyclical *Humanae Vitae* (1968) in which he condemned artificial birth control. The pope did this even though his own papal commission, people appointed to make recommendations, came to a quite different conclusion. Not only did people's respect for papal authority quickly diminish, but also many who disagreed with it began making their own decisions. They examined their consciences and decided that their actions were not sinful with regard to birth control. They realized that the pope's judgment was ultimately based on traditional natural law theory. They extended their attitudes to other moral issues.

Jim and Sue are very much concerned with saving the environment and helping others less fortunate than themselves. They realize that by so acting for others they will find their own welfare and future (see Jer 29:7). They are concerned with issues that affect the survival of the planet itself. Given the economics of their living situations, their ages, and the uncertain future, they really cannot believe that they are doing anything that is seriously wrong on a moral level by living together. They truly have the welfare of others at heart. In many respects, they believe that the Church has little to say to them in their present circumstances. Yet the Church's concern for social justice and the environment is something that resonates with them.

A similar situation exists with regard to the issue of abortion. Most people do not believe that abortion is a good thing; however, they are usually willing to allow for it in certain cases. History has shown that whether or not abortion is legal, people have them. Since unqualified people frequently perform illegal abortions in unsanitary places, a strong risk often exists of two lives being lost. For this reason, most countries allow for legal abortions.

In recent years, some bishops in the United States have provoked much debate at the time of elections when they assert that any politician who supports legalized abortion should be denied communion. In other words, some local bishops urge using a liturgical service, the one most sacred to Catholics, to reprimand publicly persons who are following their consciences. Obviously many people who believe in the freedom of conscience as articulated by Vatican II hear echoes of the Inquisition, and believe that these bishops want to make decisions for people rather than allow people to form their own consciences.

The bishops' reasoning is that both Church and State have a moral obligation to promote human life. This includes helping the poor and disadvantaged, protecting the most vulnerable, reducing the rising rates of poverty, increasing access to education and health care, and taking seriously the decision to go to war. All agree that, because abortion is not a good thing, alternatives, such as adoption, should be found. The problem arises when bishops make a blanket statement and try to enforce their viewpoint with some type of sanctions. Politicians must consider at the practical level what to do in particular cases where persons are determined to have an abortion. Should they outlaw it and make it unsafe?

Certain bishops argue that persons cannot separate political judgments from their faith. Accordingly they would extend this ban on reception of communion to those advocating embryonic stem-cell research and cloning. This "single issue" approach does not take into consideration that the same politicians might also be promoting affordable housing for the poor, programs of social justice and racial equality, health care reform, and educational initiatives. Yet the bishops stigmatize these politicians as bad persons.

In all these discussions, we see that some bishops, those who hold offices of authority, are the ones most quoted in the press. Yet other bishops often come to different practical judgments. The U.S. bishops' most recent document on political life, "Faithful Citizenship," clearly argues against making voting decisions for a candidate or a political party on the basis of a single issue, even important ones like abortion, capital punishment, or euthanasia. Here the U.S. bishops were echoing the traditional prudential judgment principle outlined by Thomas Aquinas in his treatise on the natural law, and reaffirmed more recently by Pope John Paul II in his 1995 encyclical *Evangelium Vitae* (*The Gospel of Life*). In his encyclical, the pontiff said that a politician whose own opposition to something like abortion was well known could still vote for a piece of legislation that contained abortion provisions under certain circumstances (EV #73).

Unfortunately, often qualified theologians who might have slightly different views are either not quoted or afraid to speak out in public. Rarely cited is the oldest authority on the matter. In a similar dispute about the Eucharist, St. Paul maintained the superiority of the individual conscience when he said: "Whoever, therefore, eats the bread or drinks the cup of the Lord in an unworthy manner will be answerable for the body and blood of the Lord. Examine yourselves, and only then eat of the bread and drink of the cup. For all who eat and drink without discerning the body, eat and drink judgment against themselves" (1 Cor 11:27–29). St. Paul provides a good example urging persons to follow their consciences. The persons themselves will be the ones who will answer for their actions.

What are some other controversial issues today? Certainly they include same-sex marriage, as well as sexual, gender, and racial discrimination, and economic inequalities. Not far behind are issues related to immigration, foreclosure of property, global warming, cloning, embryonic stem-cell research, and life/death issues. What price should we pay to keep people alive?

A contemporary Catholic theologian, James Bretzke, has tackled some of these issues in his book, *A Morally Complex World*.[1] The very title tells us that moral decisions are not always easy to make. Some people do not wish to invest the time or energy into making such decisions. For instance, they want simple answers to multifaceted problems. They want a "yes" or a "no" answer—no "maybes" or "buts." We might call them moral fundamentalists. Others will selectively read statements (usually out of context) of "what the pope said." Somehow they believe that if a pope (or someone in Rome) has made a statement about a subject, they're absolved from any responsibility to investigate the matter further. These attitudes were seen in the debates at Vatican II where some bishops, to make a point, would quote one pope but neglect others. The very fact that some pope over the centuries had said something was authority enough for them. This attitude showed a certain anti-intellectualism, even a cult of the papacy. It also highlighted the fact that people were often not interested in knowing the whole tradition.

The same criticism can be made of those who automatically reject any opinion given by someone in authority. They are not interested in the merits (or demerits) of the argument. Someone in authority makes a pronouncement, which immediately makes it suspect and untenable. It is impossible to say on a practical level how such persons reach a moral decision in their own lives. Sociology, psychology, or "that's what everyone is doing" might be the bases they use in talking about moral issues. Somewhere between the two extreme positions that we have outlined here, we should look for guidance in forming our consciences.

Let us take just a brief moment to look at some of the elements in the dynamic that's being discussed here. First, we need to recognize that intelligent people hold diverse views on most topics. To deny this is to live in a dream world. Second, not all opinions are of equal weight. Some are better thought out than others. Often new evidence emerges that will later change one's decision on a given subject. Third, we need to ask ourselves: "Should penalties be given to those who hold opinions contrary to those in authority who have official positions on certain matters?" The widespread abuse of the last method is certainly seen in countries that have totalitarian regimes. Should the Church imitate these governments? In every area of theology there are many different schools of thought. Can and should the official Church admit plurality in some or even many areas?

History has shown us that, over the centuries, persecution of "heretics," whether they be Catholics or Protestants, has been counterproductive. Vatican II issued a decree on religious freedom (*Dignitatis Humanae*) that affirmed the rights of people of other religions to form their own consciences in religious matters. Should not the Church extend that same liberty to those who disagree with her own official teaching on some matters? Are Church officials justified in penalizing a person who disagrees with a non-infallible teaching? Why should an office in the Vatican even exist whose officials consider it their duty to spend their time condemning other people's opinions?

SOME SUGGESTIONS

Perhaps a better approach might be for the Church to support theology in a positive manner. This would entail such things as bringing the best minds together for conferences and debates, as well as promoting discussion. To put it in ordinary language, the Church should act as the accelerator rather than the brake. In such arrangements scholars would challenge scholars. This suggestion is not unique or new. Gerald O'Collins noted in his book *Living Vatican II*, "When reforming the Congregation for the Doctrine of the Faith (hereafter CDF) on December 7, 1965, and so on the eve of the Council's closing, [Pope] Paul VI charged this institution not only with 'defending the faith,' but also with promoting Catholic teaching and theology. How far has the post-Vatican II history of the congregation been marked with shadows as well as lights in carrying out the papal mandate?"[2] Father O'Collins continues:

> Has it [the CDF] been notably successful in defending and promoting the teaching of Vatican II? Truth, as the old proverb has it, is the daughter of time. At this point, early in the twenty-first century, no well-informed answer can be given. Yet a priest who has served for many years as a consultor on the CDF admitted to me that he "wondered whether the CDF has done more harm than good." Three things might have fueled his hesitancy: a certain lack of love, justice, and balanced membership in the CDF. Where John Paul II echoed and extended Vatican II's teaching on Jesus Christ right from his first encyclical of 1979 and his stress on "the tremendous mystery of love" effectively revealed in Christ (*Redemptor Hominis* 9), some of the CDF documents seem far more concerned about truth than about love.[3]

Novitiate Library

Let us return to our original example of Jim and Sue. What is their reasoning? Most likely they consider their lifestyle a minor issue. True, they know that officially the Church condemns "living together," but so what? A lot of people also do. They believe that the existence of the planet and global warming is far more important than what they do in the bedroom. They believe that their gay and lesbian brothers and sisters should be invited to partake in the Church's life, which means receiving the Eucharist as part of the community. They believe the Church should be inclusive. They believe that the Church can and should be pluralistic without watering down any of its essential beliefs.

QUESTIONS FOR DISCUSSION

1. What should be the role of authority in the Church? Should it be juridical?
2. Do Jim and Sue have adequate reasons for following such a lifestyle?
3. Should bishops deny communion to those people whose political convictions differ from those of the ordinary teaching of the Church?
4. Can moral theology change? Should it change?
5. What is the role of the Church is promoting theological thought?

SUGGESTED READINGS

James Bretzke's book on the present state of moral theology (*A Morally Complex World*) gives a good contemporary overview of issues and theories involved in responding to moral problems. Along with coauthor and Scripture scholar, Daniel Harrington, James Keenan explores drawing upon the Bible for help in determining guidelines for making moral judgments (*Jesus and Virtue Ethics: Building Bridges*

Between New Testament Studies and Moral Theology). Other Catholic authors who write on moral theology include William Spohn (*Go and Do Likewise: Jesus and Ethics*) and John Mahoney (*The Making of Moral Theology: A Study of the Roman Catholic Tradition*). Vatican II's *Declaration on Religious Freedom* offers a challenge to extend freedom outside the Church also to those within the Church. Gerald O'Collins gives a good overview of the strong and weak points of the Vatican bureaucracy in his *Living Vatican II*.

NOTES

1. James Bretzke, *A Morally Complex World* (Collegeville, MN: Liturgical Press, 2004).

2. Gerald O'Collins, *Living Vatican II: The 21st Council for the 21st Century* (New York/Mahwah, NJ: Paulist Press, 2006), 23.

3. Ibid., 24.

CHAPTER FOUR

LAY MINISTRY AND SERVICE

Traditionally priests, brothers, and sisters have served the Catholic Church in a rather fixed and limited set of ecclesiastical roles. Most Catholics are familiar with parish priests as well as teaching brothers and sisters. Some may have encountered sisters or brothers who serve as nurses or doctors on the medical staffs of hospitals, as well as chaplains. Since Vatican II, the roles of priests, brothers, and sisters have undergone a dramatic evolution. Of course, the majority still serve in traditional roles and do so under heavier demands, due to the shortage of priests and religious, as well as the increased Catholic population in the United States. Let us take a look at one situation in which the priest shortage becomes quite evident.

CASE

Brian and Kathy were engaged to be married one December in a small, semirural town. Kathy had her heart set on getting married in the parish in which she was baptized, had received her first communion, and was confirmed. However, in the time since she was a girl, her parish had merged with another one in the neighboring town due to the shortage of priests and the changes in the Catholic population. In fact, the bishop gave the parish a new name and appointed a lay woman as the pastoral coordinator. Her role was to facilitate the ministry of the parish and arrange for priests from the area to come in on weekends to preside at the regular Sunday Masses. Fortunately, Kathy was able to contact a former teacher, who was now a Catholic priest, to celebrate her wedding. Many of her friends had searched far and wide to locate a priest available to bless their marriages.

COMMENT

From 1965 to 2008, there has been a 23 percent drop in the number of diocesan priests, and a 43 percent drop in the number of religious priests. This represents a total decrease in the number of priests in the United States of 31 percent, even while the number of Catholics has risen nearly 12 percent, from 45.6 million to 64.1 million. The decrease in the number of religious sisters is even more drastic, from 179,954 to 59,208, representing a decrease of 67 percent. Another surprising fact is that 17 percent of the parishes in the United States are now without a resident priest-pastor (3,141 out of 18,479 parishes).

It's easy to assume that the worldwide situation is better because at first glance there seems to be no shortage of priests. The total number of priests (406,411 in 2008) has diminished only an insignificant 0.3 percent from a total of 419,729 in 1965. However, one must note that *over 24 percent* of the parishes around the world have no resident priest-pastor! This is a result of a number of factors, including the distribution of priests worldwide, as well as the growing number of aged or retired priests.[1]

Clearly the Church is at a crossroads at which we must address the pastoral needs of the people of God. One excellent response would be the promotion of priestly and religious vocations. Another equally positive approach would be greater empowerment and further education of laypeople to assume more duties in the pastoral ministry of the Church. Regardless of the approach one might take, it is quite clear that several factors have affected and continue to affect how we as Catholics answer the challenges of ministry in the modern world.

One key factor that influences the decision of a young person to embrace a priestly or religious vocation is the rule of celibacy. Celibacy has traditionally been viewed as the grace that gives an individual priest, brother, or sister the freedom to dedicate his or her time to minister to all and to love all freely and equally as children of God. In giving up the privilege of having a spouse and a family, the priest or religious gains the spiritual freedom to dedicate more of his or her time to the service of the people of God. Let us take a look at one experience of a life of celibacy.

CASE

Before Frank entered the seminary, he was like most of his classmates in high school. He loved driving fast cars, listening to rock music, hanging out with friends till the late hours on weekends, and playing basketball and baseball. He dated different girls in his junior and senior years, and even went to the prom. It was only after his senior retreat that his eyes and ears were opened to the call to become a priest. He had always admired one of the associate pastors that served in his home parish because he worked tirelessly to help the homeless and jobless through his work with the Society of St. Vincent de Paul. Frank wanted to do something like that with his life, something that would really make a difference, and he decided to enter the seminary instead of going away to college with his buddies.

He knew it would be a challenge to be celibate, because he had desires like any other guy. Still, his heart told him he had a different place in life, something to give to the world other than being a parent and a husband. Today he never regrets his decision: He's a successful pastor who takes time to listen to people. He walks the streets of his inner-city parish and knows the homeless and jobless who have nowhere to go. As they call out in their need, he sees in them the face of Jesus. He has developed a true love of the people of God whom he considers his family. Fr. Frank realizes that if he had a wife and kids of his own, he wouldn't have time to serve the poor and needy of his parish the way he does. He sees his celibacy as a grace that allows him to have the time and energy to love God's people with his whole heart and soul. Being celibate might be difficult for some guys, but for him it worked just fine.

COMMENT

In response to the needs of the Church and the growing desire of married men to serve as ordained ministers, the Second Vatican Council encouraged the restoration of the lay diaconate in the dogmatic constitution *Lumen Gentium*, no. 29. Following up on this recommendation, Pope Paul VI issued his apostolic letter, *Sacrum Diaconatus Ordinem* in 1967, setting in motion the development of programs to train men to be ordained permanent deacons.[2]

Most of the candidates for the permanent diaconate are married men, chosen from among their fellow parishioners,

to serve under the direction of the bishop of the local diocese. They are given the authority to preach, baptize, and
celebrate funerals and weddings, as well as serve in other
ministries shared by laypeople. Permanent deacons are
most often assigned by the bishop to serve a term in one of
the local parishes.

One might then be led to ask, "What about the role of
women in the Church today?" A woman's traditional role in
the Catholic Church has been confined to parenting, religious life, or the single life. Throughout the years women
have played a key role in Catholic education and catechesis.
Only since Vatican II have women begun to take on more
important leadership roles in dioceses and parishes. For
example, some women hold such distinguished posts as
superintendents of Catholic education, chancellors, diocesan directors of liturgy, diocesan directors of catechetics, pastoral associates, directors of parish life, and so on. However,
in spite of these advances in key leadership roles, women are
still not allowed to be ordained as deacons or priests.

Historically, we find evidence of women serving as deacons in the early Church (1 Tim 3:8–12; Rom 16:1; Titus
2:3–5). In fact, the footnote to the New American Bible for
1 Tim 3:11 makes clear the preferred interpretation of a ref-
erence to women deacons: "This seems to refer to women
deacons but may possibly mean wives of deacons.
[However,] the former is preferred because the word is used
absolutely; [that is,] if deacons' wives were meant, a posses-
sive 'their' would be expected…[this] suggests that they too
exercised ecclesiastical functions." From a juridical perspective, the Canon Law Society of America in 1995 declared
that there is no canonical prohibition from women being
ordained to the diaconate.[3] In addition, scholars have
demonstrated that even into the twelfth century the use of

the term *ordination* was different from today: deaconesses and other women such as abbesses were deemed just as "ordained" as clergymen.[4] One might then ask, "Why have we not seen the ordination of women as deacons since Paul VI's declaration?" One answer might lie in the official position of the Holy See. Pope John Paul II, in his apostolic letter *Ordinatio Sacerdotalis* (1994), made it quite clear that by tradition the priesthood (and indirectly the diaconate) are roles for men. In that letter he states rather succinctly: "Priestly ordination, which hands on the office entrusted by Christ to his Apostles of teaching, sanctifying and governing the faithful, has in the Catholic Church from the beginning always been reserved to men alone."[5] Essentially, this statement has shut the door on the possibility of the ordination of women in the Roman Catholic Church.

On the local level, parish pastoral councils (PPCs) represent an excellent opportunity for both women and men to serve in the Church. The expertise and wisdom of laypeople with a background in business and other professions can be of great assistance to pastors, who are often quite over-extended just to meet the pastoral and sacramental demands of a parish in the United States. These councils are becoming more prevalent in dioceses across the country. In fact, from 109 dioceses and eparchies that responded in a recent survey, "an average of 85% of parishes are reported to have established PPCs."[6] The types of activities in which these PPCs are involved can vary widely, but the American bishops, to different degrees, have recommended that activities include "pastoral planning, broad consultation with parishioners to elicit hopes and concerns of the community, empowering parishioners to carry out plan objectives, regular prayer and faith sharing, coordinating or overseeing parish activities/events, reporting on parish activities/events, and carrying out or implementing parish activities/events."[7] All of these recommendations point to a growing empowerment of the laity to influence the direction of the management and pastoral policies of their parishes.

In addition, quite a few lay groups have formed in the Catholic Church in reaction to various events, changes, and crises. Most of these concerns center on such controversial issues as sexual abuse by clergy, women's ordination, homosexuality, and the celebration of the Mass. Some examples of these groups or organizations are Voice of the Faithful (VOTF), Catholics United for the Faith (CUF), Roman Catholic Womenpriests, Call to Action, Dignity, and Survivors' Network of those Abused by Priests (SNAP). Although these lay associations are not officially recognized by the Church, they express authentic concerns of Catholics around the United States. Certainly, they are one indication of the signs of the times since they represent "the joys and the hopes, the griefs and the anxieties"[8] of the people of this era. Furthermore, they remind us how important it is for all Catholics to be informed and active in the Church in the modern world because "the Church has always had the duty of scrutinizing the signs of the times and of interpreting them in the light of the Gospel."[9]

One way to respond to the problems and needs of the modern world is to dedicate time as a volunteer in a service organization of the Catholic Church. These are not limited to the more traditional altar societies and fraternal organizations, but include a whole range of opportunities, even living in the inner city with other laypeople who volunteer one or more years to serve the poor. Some examples of this vast spectrum of lay service organizations are the Society of St. Vincent de Paul, Catholic Charities USA, Catholic Relief

Services, Catholic Youth Organization (CYO), and the Jesuit Volunteer Corps. Besides these larger national and international efforts, some dioceses and religious congregations have developed extensive local service opportunities. Catholics can consult their diocesan office for more possible ways to serve in the region in which they live.

Some Catholics often wonder how we might relate better to people of other faith traditions. Several lay organizations provide opportunities for interreligious dialogue and ecumenical ministry, besides serving the sacramental and pastoral needs of Catholic parishioners. Because marriages in the U.S. Catholic Church frequently involve different religions, these organizations strive to help engaged and married couples deal with issues of faith and practice that can be a source of disagreement between them. Some examples of these types of efforts include Marriage Encounter, Engaged Encounter, and Retrouvaille.

Many Catholics are apprehensive about discussing or confronting the political and social issues of our times. Often, people feel a great tension between political and religious themes in homilies and catechetics. Some would even claim that politics has no place in the pulpit. Here is one such case.

CASE

Jack and Dorothy have been faithful Catholics all their lives. Each Sunday they attend their local parish and participate actively as lectors and eucharistic ministers. In general, they are very happy with the way Fr. Bob, the pastor, administrates the parish. However, one thing disturbs them a great deal: Fr. Bob brings politics into the homily almost every

Sunday. He is constantly pointing out his concerns about living conditions in the local state prison that he visits each week, as well as the injustice of capital punishment. Jack has written the bishop to complain, but the bishop has refused to take any action to change things. Both Jack and Dorothy are staunch supporters of the death penalty. They believe in an eye for an eye and a tooth for a tooth. Because of this, they have threatened to go to another parish, but Fr. Bob still refuses to change his ways.

COMMENT

Such an experience of discomfort may point to a lack of knowledge and clarity about our Catholic social teaching. Because of this, many parishes provide adult education classes and discussion groups to help laypeople learn more about key documents about the social teaching of the Catholic Church. These include papal encyclicals and USCCB pastoral statements, as well as writings by Catholic moral theologians. One of the most recent (November 2007) USCCB documents, *Forming Consciences for Faithful Citizenship: A Call to Political Responsibility from the Catholic Bishops of the United States*, addresses a vast range of current social and political issues. These include seven thematic areas that we as Catholics are asked to consider: right to life and dignity of the human person; call to family, community, and participation; rights and responsibilities; option for the poor and vulnerable; dignity of work and the rights of workers; solidarity; and caring for God's creation.

The bishops are quite explicit regarding the right to life and the dignity of the human person: "Society has a duty to defend life against violence and to reach out to victims of crime. Yet our nation's continued reliance on the death penalty cannot be justified."[10] This is just one example of how we as Catholics need to constantly inform our consciences in order to make good, moral decisions as faithful citizens of this country. Of course, this should not be news to us. We might recall that in 1963 Blessed Pope John XXIII wrote, "[Each of us] has the right to life, to bodily integrity, and to the means which are suitable for the proper development of life; these are primarily food, clothing, shelter, rest, medical care, and, finally, the necessary social services."[11] Our role as Catholics is clearly one of service to God and neighbor: to work for the common good, that is, "the sum total of social conditions which allow people, either as groups or as individuals, to reach their fulfillment more fully and more easily."[12]

QUESTIONS FOR DISCUSSION

1. How should we resolve the shortage of priests in the United States?
2. What should be the role of women in the Church today? Should women be ordained?
3. Should celibacy be optional for diocesan priests?
4. What should be the role of parish pastoral councils?
5. How can we respond to social and political issues as people of faith?

SUGGESTED READINGS

Georgetown University's Center for Applied Research in the Apostolate has an excellent Web site that presents current demographic data about the shortage of priests and the Catholic population in general. It can be accessed at http://cara.georgetown.edu/bulletin/index.htm. In addition, many excellent documents have been written and developed by the USCCB itself. One that is very thorough and deals with U.S. political and social issues is entitled *Forming Consciences for Faithful Citizenship: A Call to Political Responsibility from the Catholic Bishops of the United States*. It can be accessed on the Internet at http://www.usccb.org/bishops/FCStatement.pdf. Finally, a useful document for those interested in learning more about diocesan and parish pastoral councils is the *Committee on the Laity Report on Diocesan and Parish Pastoral Councils* (http://www.usccb.org/laity/summary.shtml).

NOTES

1. Center for Applied Research in the Apostolate (CARA), Georgetown University, retrieved July 15, 2008, from http://cara.georgetown.edu/bulletin/index.htm.

2. *Sacrum Diaconatus Ordinem*, June 18, 1967.

3. *The Canonical Implication of Ordaining Women to the Permanent Diaconate*, report of an ad hoc committee to the Canon Law Society of America, presented to the 57th annual meeting (Washington, DC: Canon Law Society of America, 1995).

4. Gary Macy, "The Ordination of Women in the Early Middle Ages," *Theological Studies* 61 (2000): 481–507.

5. *Ordinatio Sacerdotalis*, no. 1.

6. USCCB, Committee on the Laity Report on Diocesan and Parish Pastoral Councils (March 12, 2004). Secretariat of Laity, Marriage, Family Life, and Youth.

7. Ibid.

8. *Gaudium et Spes*, no. 1.

9. Ibid., no. 4.

10. USCCB, *Forming Consciences for Faithful Citizenship: A Call to Political Responsibility from the Catholic Bishops of the United States*, November 2007, no. 69.

11. *Pacem in Terris*, no. 11.

12. *Catechism of the Catholic Church*, no. 1906.

CHAPTER FIVE

MAKING SENSE OF CYBER-CATHOLICISM

The Church in the technological era faces many challenges and obstacles to its effective mission. The challenges include the ever-evolving communication media and the immediacy of access to information. The obstacles involve the ethical and appropriate use of human technology for the common good. In this chapter we will examine some of the crucial issues that being Catholic in the technological age entails, as well as envision how Catholics in the future might address emergent concerns as they surface. Many of these issues are taken up quite thoroughly and eloquently in the recent documents of the Pontifical Council for Social Communications.

Technology is a means of communication, a product meant to be placed at the service of humanity for the common good. To what extent do technological advances help or hinder a life of faith as a Catholic? How might we as Catholics reshape our use or misuse of these tools in the future?

The use of the Internet and other means of modern communication have reframed the way in which we as Catholics understand the world around us. Because ideas and images are so readily available and rapidly sent and received, we must take care to use these tools well with concern for the emotional, moral, and spiritual well-being of others and ourselves. In addition, we should take into account the wide range of cultural values and religious beliefs that are expressed via modern media.[1]

As Catholics, we understand that technology has the capacity to enhance our work, another set of tools to support us in our efforts to contribute to the common good. We must take care, however, to not allow technology to take control of us or manipulate humanity in such a way as to dehumanize ourselves or others. Furthermore, if technology eliminates opportunities for employment or diminishes our motivation to work, it can become the enemy of humanity rather than our ally, reducing us to the level of an object or slave.[2]

When reflecting upon an ethical approach to the use of the Internet, we as Catholics might do well to begin with the image of Jesus Christ as the perfect communicator.[3] Since the primary purpose of the Internet is to communicate, our intention should be to share and retrieve information in a way that conveys our love for one another in the Spirit of Christ. We then might ask ourselves if our use of the Internet and other media is contributing to our true development as human beings, as well as assisting us and others to be faithful to our call to follow Jesus Christ, the Perfect Communicator.[4] In this chapter we will attempt to indicate the pertinent ethical criteria to assist us in deciding what is appropriate and helpful in our use of the Internet based upon truly Christian values.[5] An example of an extreme case will allow us to examine the issues involved.

CASE

Fr. Joe was a well-respected pastor of a large, vibrant, Catholic parish in the suburbs of a large city in the Midwest. The parishioners loved Fr. Joe's homilies and humor, and his availability to help them in times of illness and grief. From all appearances he was an ideal, outgoing priest, who served the people well and who loved his vocation. However, Fr. Joe had a hidden side to his personality: he was addicted to viewing pornography over the Internet.

One day a parish staff member surprised Fr. Joe by interrupting him and discovered that he was viewing inappropriate photographs on his computer. The staff member, in shock, consulted with the diocesan offices and reported the case to the human resources department there. Later, the bishop called Fr. Joe in, confronted him about his addiction, and asked him to consider a treatment program to help him overcome this problem. Fr. Joe agreed and, with the help of therapy and spiritual direction, has dealt with his addiction and been able to return to active ministry, where he leads a more balanced celibate lifestyle without resorting to the use of Internet pornography.

COMMENT

How do we make sense of our lives as Catholics in this age of the Internet and cyberspace? One area upon which we should reflect is the appropriate and ethical use of the Internet as individuals and as a society. Like all inventions, the Internet is a true gift to be used for the common good, to promote and sustain our lives as the family of humanity. The use of the Internet for pornographic purposes clearly goes against the notion of a true gift that would promote and sustain our lives. Furthermore, since pornography is often a search for self-centered personal gratification, it can contribute to undermining the quality of human life and, in particular, Catholic marriage and family life.[6] Catholics need to possess certain virtues when deciding how to appropriately use the Internet for work or recreation: these include prudence, justice, fortitude, courage, and temperance.[7]

Of course, one age-old approach that many have found beneficial is the virtuous advice of St. Paul who said, "Do not be overcome by evil, but overcome evil with good" (Rom 12:21). This is often echoed in popular sports culture by the statement: the best defense is a good offense. Put simply: if we are busy doing good things, we simply do not have time to do evil things. "Pornography and sadistic violence debase sexuality, corrode human relationships, exploit individuals—especially women and young people—undermine marriage and family life, foster anti-social behavior and weaken the moral fiber of society itself."[8]

Besides the temptation to use the Internet to access pornographic material, some Catholics are also confronted with the question of proper use of copyrighted matter. Since the Internet provides an overabundance of information for professionals, students, and others, care must be taken to respect the ownership of the printed matter of others, and to respect national and international copyright laws. Some have made the mistake of cutting and pasting whole stories from the Internet to incorporate in their own publications without seeking permission of the authors, only to find themselves later faced with lawsuits. We can avoid these kinds of tragedies by attributing or referencing the work of others appropriately in our school and professional work.[9]

In addition, Catholics, and all men and women of good-will, need to respect the rights and privileges of others in the use of the Internet. With the proliferation of information in cyberspace, Catholics need to carefully select what they read and write to consider the potential effect that written or posted material might have on the viewer or listener. Another consideration is to balance the right to freedom of expression and exchange of information with people's right to privacy, decency, and basic human values.[10]

Given the plethora of Web sites and the ease with which one can create and post information, Catholics must be cautious in accepting information from the Internet as true doctrine. Some Web sites may call themselves Catholic but lack any official recognition by the Vatican, diocese, or religious congregation. The authority that Web sites bear on our lives as Catholics depends upon the agency or organization that promotes this information. Since the Church recognizes the freedom of expression of individuals and groups, varying opinions (some eccentric or even idiosyncratic) abound in Web sites that present themselves as Catholic. Individuals must use their discretion when reading or listening to information presented through this medium.[11]

One possible solution to the confusion surrounding which Internet sites express the official Catholic position would be to have a single, recognized source, such as one sponsored by the United States Conference of Catholic Bishops. An arrangement of this type would allow those who do not know the Church's stance on diverse topics to understand better arguments for and against the official position.[12]

People make use of e-mail quite commonly at home, school, work, and even on the road. Most recognize the convenience, immediacy, and beauty of communicating their thoughts and feelings via electronic mail. However, all of the positive qualities of e-mail can be negated when expressions of anger, impersonal language, and dehumanization creep into the correspondence. Let us take a look at one example to illuminate this reality.

CASE

Jackie's work involves a great deal of e-mail correspondence for clients in the bank where she works. One day she received a customer complaint about a mistake in her monthly checking-account statement. Jackie had slept badly the night before and was already on edge. She zipped off a quick response to the customer and neglected to proofread it before hitting the send button. Later in the day, after her second cup of coffee, she went back and reread this e-mail and realized that she had misspelled the customer's name and expressed anger at the complaint. There was no way she could retract the e-mail once it was sent. Now Jackie fears there may be reprisals for her e-mail attitude once the customer receives it. She is afraid her boss may write her up negatively on her annual performance appraisal because of her short-fused temper.

COMMENT

Patience and care are important for ensuring that e-mail messages are not laden with an emotional charge that the sender will regret later. Many experienced e-mail users compose their e-mails and send them later after they have had time to "cool off" if they are dealing with tense or difficult cases. After rereading the e-mails and editing them to guarantee their respectful tone and content, only then do professionals send the e-mails to the intended recipients. In addition, much caution needs to be employed to protect the confidentiality of the recipient. Hence, one must exercise great discretion when sending copies to others, making sure that only those immediately involved in a situation are participants in the communication. The risk in sending copies to others is the possibility of scandal, defamation of character, or the spreading of rumor.[13]

In addition to the problem of the emotional content in e-mails, Catholics should also be concerned about their general tone. Because we value each person as a child of God, we have the obligation to treat the recipients of e-mails with respect and dignity, so that we never dehumanize them or treat them impersonally. The Internet is a tool meant for the common good of social communication. Because of this, e-mails should maintain a tone that reflects our Catholic beliefs and values: treating one another as made in the image and likeness of God, our Creator.

This in turns leads to a consideration of the great digital divide that the Internet can create between those who have access to use of the Internet and those who do not. We must take care to not heighten the cultural and social divisions that already exist by making the Internet an instrument of privilege and oppression.[14] "In particular, the question of how to close the digital divide between the 'information rich' and the 'information poor' requires urgent attention in its technical, educational, and cultural aspects."[15]

The Internet provides several other useful techniques of social communication such as texting, blogging, and wikis. These too, however, bring with them miscommunication and misinformation. Take, for example, the following situation among young adults.

CASE

Caitlin and Dave attend a Catholic university in the Midwest. They are usually in different classes because she's a communications major and he's in engineering. During the course of each day, while they go to their separate classes, they enjoy keeping in touch with one another by text messaging. They are very much in love and like to keep in close contact. Even though some of their professors have made it clear in their syllabi that this is not allowed during class time, they do it anyway. One day, during a quiz, Caitlin's professor caught her in the act of texting. He made her turn in her quiz and gave her an F on it. Needless to say she was very upset and tried to explain that she was not cheating, but only talking with her boyfriend Dave who was in his engineering class. The professor pointed out to her that text messaging was not allowed in his classes under any circumstances for this very reason.

COMMENT

Once again the Internet can provide effective and immediate means of communication between individuals. However, as Catholics we must question the appropriateness of its use in certain contexts, such as that of these college students. When texting, blogging, or wiki-posting interfere with normal, face-to-face interaction, they clearly do not enhance but detract from meaningful and humanizing communication. In fact, the amount of information-exchange taking place can create an overload and cause difficulties in processing that information.[16] One must weigh the effect and personal value that texting, blogging, and wiki-posting have on our lives as Catholics. We might do well to ask ourselves: Are these tools of the Internet improving the quality of our relationships? Are these techniques of communication closing us off from dealing with people directly? Are these the best means by which to communicate and in the appropriate or optimal context?[17]

In addition to e-mail, texting, blogging, and wikis, the Internet provides several other opportunities for social communication. At first glance, online dating, chatrooms, and instant messaging all seem to be benevolent tools of communication, but upon closer reflection, some problems might arise even in these applications. To grasp this more fully, we turn to another case in which some concerns or doubts enter the picture.

CASE

Ralph and Jane are both widowed Catholics. In their frustration to make new single, older friends, they subscribed to an online dating service that guaranteed to help people find their true soul mate. After some initial chatting with potential dates, they finally met each other and set a time and place to go out to dinner together. Both of them are having second thoughts and guilt feelings about this way of meeting new friends. They are wondering what the Church would say about their dating in this way.

COMMENT

One of the benefits of the Internet is its ability to help people communicate rapidly, efficiently, and almost immediately. Many younger, and even older couples, are searching for friends and acquaintances via the Internet. This brings up some challenging ethical questions. One is in regard to the impersonal nature of the Internet, which can be used to help bring people together or to push them further apart. Some uses of the Internet are self-seeking and narcissistic, encouraging users to enter into a materialistic approach to life in the modern world. Catholics must take great care to avoid dehumanizing themselves and others if they make use of this medium to meet others and sustain relationships.

Another danger of this type of use of the Internet is the tendency to immediately gratify oneself. In addition, when people return and return to anonymously chatting or playing roles via the Internet in chatrooms, they run the risk of demeaning themselves and others as human beings in the process. Catholics and other people of good-will ought to refrain from participating in this misuse of the Internet. Online dating services, chatrooms, and instant messages should be looked upon as occasional or rare methods of communicating with friends and relatives.[18] A good measure of this use of the Internet might be to ask oneself: Is this enhancing my friendships and relationships with others or doing them harm? One such example of a positive use of the Internet would be to keep in communication with relatives who live a great distance away or overseas, using either e-mails or instant messaging. This type of communication can help maintain and even strengthen the relationship one has with family members when the high cost of travel prohibits face-to-face reunions.

Finally, our attention is drawn to questions about virtual attendance at Mass and the celebration of the sacraments via electronic media. An example may serve to better envision the issues involved here.

CASE

Mary has been away from the sacraments for over ten years because of deep remorse and guilt over an abortion she had when she was younger. She's afraid to go to confession because of what the priest might think of her and say to her. When she was young, she had some confessors severely reprimand her for her sexual behavior. Mary is wondering if there might not be a way to go to confession over the Internet, like in a chatroom. She would feel much more comfortable than going to confess her serious sins face-to-face with a priest.

COMMENT

Virtual reality cannot replace the sacraments. Since our experience of Christ is in the Church, the people of God, sacraments take place in a face-to-face manner. The community at prayer and worship celebrates the real presence of Christ in the Eucharist. Nothing can replace "the real-world interaction with other persons of faith."[19] The use of the Internet can serve as a supplement to the celebration of the sacraments. Catholics can find there an overabundance of prayers, Scripture, reflection, and information for their private or family study. In addition, the media are a wonderful way to reach the homebound and the sick with the Word of God, as well as to reach rural and more isolated groups of Catholics who hunger for Christ.[20]

Another purposeful use of the Internet in the Catholic Church is to evangelize. Much like other means of communication, the Internet now plays a key role in the evangelization and catechetical efforts by parishes, retreat centers, dioceses, and religious congregations and organizations.

The Internet serves as an instrument of re-evangelization and new evangelization in a changing world. It does so not only with the written word, but also with visual representations of our world and our faith as Catholics.[21]

QUESTIONS FOR DISCUSSION

1. What should be the guiding principles of our use of cyberspace?
2. When and how is it appropriate to make new friends via the Internet?
3. How should Catholic parents monitor their children's use of the Internet?
4. How can the use of the Internet help us in our faith and the practice of it?
5. How might we as Catholics reshape our use or misuse of these tools in the future?

SUGGESTED READINGS

Once again, James Bretzke's book *A Morally Complex World* gives a good contemporary overview of issues and theories involved in responding to moral problems. For those looking for a shorter reading, the USCCB's *Your Family and Cyberspace* at http://www.usccb.org/comm/cyberspace.shtml provides an excellent summary of the use of the Internet for parents. On another note, *Ethics in Internet* is a more thorough study of the ethical use of the Internet in general and can be accessed from the Vatican Web site at http://www.vatican.va/. Finally, for a fuller development of ethical considerations regarding pornography in general, one might consult the document *Pornography and Violence in the Communications Media: A Pastoral Response*, also at the Vatican Web site.

NOTES

1. *Aetatis Novae: Pastoral Instruction on Social Communications on the Twentieth Anniversary of Communio et Progressio* (1992), 4. Except for *Laborem Exercens,* this and the remaining notes come from documents issued by the Pontifical Council for Social Communications.

2. *Laborem Exercens* (1981), 5.

3. *Communio et Progressio* (1971), 11.

4. *Ethics in Internet* (2002), 1.

5. *Aetatis Novae,* 27.

6. *Pornography and Violence in the Communications Media: A Pastoral Response* (1989), 16.

7. *The Church and Internet* (2002), 12.

8. *Pornography and Violence in the Communications Media: A Pastoral Response,* 10.

9. *Ethics in Internet,* 6.

10. *Pornography and Violence in the Communications Media: A Pastoral Response,* 21.

11. *The Church and Internet,* 8.

12. Ibid., 11.

13. *Ethics in Internet,* 6.

14. Ibid., 10.

15. Ibid., 10.

16. Ibid., 13.

17. Ibid., 15.

18. Ibid., 7.

19. *The Church and Internet,* 9.

20. Ibid., 5.

21. *Aetatis Novae,* 11.

CHAPTER 6

BEING CATHOLIC IN A POST–9/11 WORLD

The tragic, shocking events of September 11, 2001, marked a turning point in the history of the United States. Never again as Americans would we or could we presume our relative freedom from terrorism or insurgency again. This shift in perspective has affected us not only politically, but socially and religiously as well. These events and others have fostered both a fear of terrorism and a fear of foreigners (xenophobia) that marks our life in the post–9/11 world. In this chapter we will explore a range of the moral, spiritual, and religious ramifications of this paradigm shift. What does it mean to be a Catholic in a post–9/11 world? What could it mean for the future of the Catholic Church in the United States?

The destruction of the twin towers of the World Trade Center on the morning of September 11, 2001, serves as a shocking reminder of our collective shortsightedness as a country. Prior to that time many assumptions dominated our political, social, and religious decision making. Nevertheless, since we believe that God can draw good from apparent evil (Rom 8:28), the American Church must now broaden the scope of our shared vision to include the entire world. We are obligated to see the interconnectedness of nations and peoples from around the world. What occurs in

Afghanistan or Iraq directly affects the tenor and quality of our lives here in the United States, from the high price of gas to the way we check in for a flight at the airport. As Catholics, what should be our role given this dramatic shift in perspective?

To answer this question, let us first take a look at the situation of one family and how this has impacted their faith life.

CASE

Since 1995, John and Susie Adamson had lived and worked peacefully and happily in New York. John was an insurance broker whose corporation was housed in the World Trade Center. Susie taught in a suburban Catholic elementary school. Since childhood, both John and Susie had been brought up as good, practicing Catholics, attending Catholic elementary schools, high schools, and colleges. John graduated with an MBA from Fordham University in 1982. Susie earned her New York elementary teaching certificate there in 1980. They were blessed with two beautiful children, Jamie and Jackie, who were still in grade school at time of the disaster.

On that fateful day, John died heroically helping his colleagues gain access to the stairways and checking and rechecking all the cubicles of his office for possible workers who had lagged behind. Unfortunately, John did not make it out. He was overcome by smoke and could not reach the stairwell in time to exit the building before the collapse. Susie was already at school when the 9/11 tragedy occurred. She received cellphone messages as she began the morning lessons around 8:25 a.m. Over the phone, John and Susie expressed their love for one another and said their last goodbyes shortly after. Susie never saw John again alive and has been suffering from psychological trauma and stress ever since. With the help of therapy and medication, she was eventually able to return to her teaching job, but has never been able to forget or forgive the terrorists who perpetrated this act of violence. Even worse, as a Catholic, Susie carries a sense of guilt that she ought to be able to forgive, but emotionally cannot bring herself to that point. Jamie and Jackie managed to finish high school and are now away at college, but find themselves locked into the party circuit. They feel trapped in a cycle of attempting to dull the pain of the loss of their father with drug and alcohol use, as well as sporadic and unsatisfying sexual exploits. Every time they see a student on campus that looks even remotely Middle Eastern, both Jamie and Jackie feel a deep rage welling up. Much like their mother, they cannot bring themselves to forgive those who killed their father and thousands of other people.

COMMENT

As Catholics, just what should be our relationship to non-Christians, especially in the light of the 9/11 tragedy? As far back as 1985, Pope John Paul II was reaching out to non-Christians when he accepted an invitation to address over 100,000 young Muslims in Morocco. At that time, he expressed love and welcome to a people who share a common ancestry in the faith of Abraham. This increasing sensitivity to Islam points to the manner in which Catholics should approach others who are outside our Church.

The following year (1986), the same Pope John Paul II continued his effort to reach out to all religious leaders at Assisi. There with the Dalai Lama and other religious leaders from around the world, the Holy Father prayed for peace. Later that same year, he followed up on this with his Christmas address of December 22, 1986, by pointing out that the Spirit "is mysteriously present in the heart of every person."[1] This great mystery serves as the basis of our faith as Catholics when relating to others who are outside our Church.

In spite of these important gestures, it would appear that a great chasm still exists between them and us. In fact, as Catholics we are still left with questions about how to reconcile the differences that exist between us and others who are outside the Church. In an effort to grapple with the issues involved, Pope Benedict XVI gave a lecture in Regensburg, Germany, on September 12, 2006, that addressed some of the differences in faith and reason between Christians and Muslims. This controversial address triggered a response worldwide by leaders of many faiths. In particular, one month later to the day, thirty-eight leaders of Islam wrote an open letter to His Holiness to address the issues raised there and to establish some common ground for dialogue between Islam and Christianity. They proposed that the basis of such future dialogue be the love of God and the love of neighbor. As a matter of fact, not only do Islam and Christianity share the same divine origin and Abrahamic heritage, but they also espouse the same two greatest commandments. In their "Open Letter to His Holiness Pope Benedict XVI," the leaders of Islam stated:

> We share your desire for frank and sincere dialogue, and recognize its importance in an increasingly interconnected world. Upon this sincere and frank dialogue we hope to continue to build peaceful and friendly relationships based upon mutual respect,

justice, and what is common in essence in our shared Abrahamic tradition, particularly "the two greatest commandments" in Mark 12:29–31 (and, in varying form, in Matthew 22:37–40), that, "…the Lord our God is One Lord; / And thou shalt love the Lord thy God with all thy heart, and with all thy soul, and with all thy understanding, and with all thy strength: this is the first commandment. / And the second commandment is like, namely this, Thou shalt love thy neighbor as thyself. There is none other commandment greater than these."[2]

A year later, on October 13, 2007, 138 Islam leaders issued yet another statement to renew the call to come together as Christians and Muslims. In their document entitled "A Common Word between Us and You," they stated: "Thus in obedience to the Holy Qur'an, we as Muslims invite Christians to come together with us on the basis of what is common to us, which is also what is most essential to our faith and practice: the *Two Commandments* of love." Later in the document, they based this statement on the commandment found in the Qur'an in which God enjoins all Muslims "to issue the following call to Christians (and Jews—the People of the Scripture): 'Say: O People of the Scripture! Come to a common word between us and you: that we shall worship none but God, and that we shall ascribe no partner unto Him, and that none of us shall take others for lords beside God.'"[3] This statement represents a radical move on the part of the leaders of Islam to recognize the common word that is our mutual love of God. Christians may see this summons as a call to live out the Gospel in Spirit and in truth, by establishing a relationship with our Muslim neighbors based upon the law of love.

From the Old Testament, we learn how difficult it was even in ancient times for the people of Israel to accept that the one true God could be working in the lives of those who were not part of their faith tradition. Gerald O'Collins, SJ, in his book *Salvation for All: God's Other Peoples* asserts that "it is worth observing how the stories of such divine dealings with two 'outsiders,' the widow of Zarephath and Naaman the Syrian, could prove so offensive to the 'insiders' or members of God's chosen people."[4] God works not only in mysterious but also purposeful ways to bring all people to faith, even those who are outside the Jewish religion. Truly our own Jewish and Christian scriptural traditions point out ways in which God has chosen outsiders as a way to reveal the Word and to bring about salvation for all people.

Frequently we Catholics make comments or even statements about other religions that are quite stereotypical in their nature. For example, we might be caught saying, "All Muslims think the same way," or "Evangelical Christians are all dogmatic fundamentalists," or "Buddhists really don't have a Supreme Being as part of their belief." Given such a tendency to prejudge non-Catholics, how do we deal with issues of cultural pluralism and freedom of religion? First of all, we might begin by recognizing that no person or circumstance is or ever can be "outside" of Christ: God's life and love is available to all through Christ.[5] If we have just such an outlook of acceptance and inclusion, we are more adequately prepared to embrace the cultural diversity of the Catholic Church itself, as well as embrace the way in which God is laboring to bring salvation to all people in Christ. This is the great mystery that we embrace as a catholic—a universal—Church. Pope John Paul II, in his encyclical *Redemptoris Missio* ("The Mission of the Redeemer"), insisted that "the Spirit's presence and activity affect not only individuals but also society and history, peoples, cultures and religions."[6]

With the current influx of Asian and Latin American immigrants into the United States, many Catholics today feel unprepared to adapt to the changing cultural makeup of their parish communities. The rate of immigration combined with the reduced birth rate among American Catholics has heightened the process of change in the pew. All of these factors contribute to the confusion and tension of the worshiping community at Sunday liturgies. How do we adapt to cultural diversity especially in such a historically immigrant country as the United States? Here is one such case.

CASE

Sara, the director of catechetics at a large urban parish, struggles with the diversity of cultural groups she serves. She directs and trains Filipino, Vietnamese, Mexican, and Central American catechists for the first communion program. The parish celebrates over four hundred first communions for children during Easter time each year. Sara and her team are challenged to coordinate the content of the classes, as well as the actual liturgies, because of conflicting expectations of the children's families, based upon their own experiences of the way they used to do things back home. The customs and practices of the faith vary a great deal among them, as well as the languages that people speak when they worship. Sara and her colleagues are constantly bombarded and overwhelmed by the pressure of the many demands and complaints by parents to incorporate their cultural religious style and expressions into the lessons and actual ceremonies. At the end of each school year, Sara feels like resigning from her staff position and giving up her ministry as a master catechist.

COMMENT

Some Catholics are confused about their role in regard to the new immigrants among us. Most recognize a growing need to adapt our catechesis to the needs and customs of different cultures. And so they ask, "What should be our role as Catholic parishioners with the arrival of so many people from Vietnam, Mexico, the Philippines, and other Asian and Latin American countries?" Many react out of fear of losing their roles or feel threatened because people's customs and beliefs appear to be different from what they are accustomed. We learn in Scripture that "there is no fear in love, but perfect love casts out fear; for fear has to do with punishment" (1 John 4:18).

Perhaps we might turn again to the late Pope John Paul II, in his *Annual Message for World Migration Day* in 1995, when he chose Jesus as the model of the immigrant. He began his message with a passage from Scripture: " 'I was a stranger and you welcomed me' (Matthew 25:35). Today the illegal migrant comes before us like that 'stranger' in whom Jesus asks to be recognized. To welcome him and to show him solidarity is a duty of hospitality and fidelity to Christian identity itself."

Together with all Christians (and Muslims for that matter), we Catholics are called to love our neighbor as ourselves. But we might ask ourselves the same question that prompted the parable of the Good Samaritan—Just who are our neighbors? Certainly they include those recently arrived in this country, as well as those who were born on our native soil.

Catholic leaders across the United States have responded quite clearly to this question within the last several years. For example, on November 15, 2000, the United States Conference of Catholic Bishops issued a pastoral letter entitled, "Welcoming the Stranger among Us: Unity in Diversity." The very title makes it clear that our response to newcomers from other countries (our new neighbors) should be the type of welcome mentioned in Matthew's Gospel: we strive for unity in a culturally diverse Church.

Several years later, on March 21, 2006, the California Conference of Catholic Bishops, in its statement on immigration reform, also asked the question, "And who is my neighbor?"[7] In that document they pointed out that, if we take the notion of a "good neighbor" seriously, then we must "implore our national legislators to give us a law that reforms immigration in a way that protects human dignity and promotes the common good."

And three months later, on June 15, 2006, Bishop William Skylstad, then president of the USCCB, insisted that "our immigration laws should be just and humane and reflect the values—fairness, opportunity, and compassion— upon which our nation, a nation of immigrants, was built." According to Bishop Skylstad, a flawed immigration system produces the following results: "Families are divided, migrants are exploited and abused by smugglers and human traffickers, and, in some cases, men, women and children who attempt to come here in search of a better life perish in the American desert and on the seas."[8] The time has come for freedom-loving Americans to become good neighbors again.

More than forty years ago, Pope John XXIII mentioned that history is the teacher of life.[9] Most certainly, it is important to recall our collective history in areas of crucial concern in order to learn how to build up a Church that will be even more relevant for future generations. The Apostle Paul appealed to the Greeks who worshiped "the unknown God" (Acts 17:22–33). According to Gerald O'Collins, Paul's catechetical perspective used the unknown God of the Greeks as a way to talk about "the unknown Christ who has been and is effective everywhere, for everyone, and in the history of all cultures and religions—albeit often hiddenly. He may be unknown, but never absent."[10] This indeed should be our approach as Catholics even now in the third millennium: to help others encounter the Christ who is present among us as we strive to embrace the diversity of cultural expression in our Church.

QUESTIONS FOR DISCUSSION

1. What should be our response as Catholics to acts of terrorism?
2. How should we as Catholics deal with undocumented immigrants?
3. Is there salvation for people who are not Catholic or even Christian?
4. How can we forgive those who have committed acts of violence?
5. What kind of relationship should we as Catholics have with those of other faiths?
6. How can we achieve unity in the Catholic Church with people from so many cultural backgrounds?

SUGGESTED READINGS

Similar to themes in earlier chapters, a discussion on issues in the post–9/11 world might begin with the documents of the Second Vatican Council, especially the documents on the Church (*Lumen Gentium*) and the Church today (*Gaudium et*

Spes). One particularly helpful book in dealing with how to respond to people of non-Christian faiths is Gerald O'Collins's book *Salvation for All: God's Other Peoples*. Lisa Sowle Cahill has published *Love Your Enemies: Discipleship, Pacifism, and Just War Theory*. Finally, check out the USCCB's Web site for pastoral letters regarding terrorism, violence, immigration, the dignity of life, and many other contemporary social and political issues (http://www.nccbuscc.org/).

NOTES

1. *Acta Apostolicae Sedis* 79 (1987), 1082–90, at 1089. The full text of the address was published by the Secretariat of Non-Christians (renamed in 1988 the Pontifical Council for Interreligious Dialogue), in *Bulletin* 64/22/1 (1987), 54–62. In addition, the key passages are found in J. Neuner and J. Dupuis, eds., *The Christian Faith*, 7th ed. (New York: Alba House, 2001), nos. 1049–52.

2. http://www.monasticdialog.com/a.php?id=789.

3. The entire document may be read online at http://www.timesonline.co.uk/multimedia/archive/00218/Open_letter_from__M_218459a.pdf.

4. Gerald O'Collins, SJ, *Salvation for All: God's Other Peoples* (New York: Oxford, 2008), 29–30.

5. Ibid., 215.

6. *Redemptoris Missio* (1990), 28.

7. http://www.justiceforimmigrants.org/files/CCCStatementonImmigration.pdf

8. http://www.usccb.org/bishops/immigrationreform.shtml.

9. "Opening Speech to the Council," in W. M. Abbott and J. Gallagher, *The Documents of Vatican II* (New York: America Press, 1966), 712.

10. O'Collins, 219.

REFERENCES

Aetatis Novae ("The Dawn of a New Era")—1992 Pastoral Instruction on Social Communication from the Pontifical Council for Social Communications.

Apostolicam Actuositatem ("Apostolic Activity")—1965 Decree of Vatican II on the apostolate of the laity.

Church and Internet—1992 document from the Pontifical Council for Social Communications.

Communio et Progressio ("Unity and Advancement")—1971 pastoral instruction on the means of social communication, written by order of the Second Vatican Council.

Dei Verbum ("The Word of God")—Vatican II's 1995 dogmatic constitution on divine revelation.

Dignitatis Humanae ("Human Dignity")—Vatican II's 1965 declaration on the right of persons and communities to social and civil and religious freedom in matters religious.

Ethics in Internet—1992 document from the Pontifical Council for Social Communications.

Evangelium Vitae ("The Gospel of Life")—1995 encyclical of Pope John Paul II on the value and inviolability of human life.

Gaudium et Spes ("Joy and Hope")—Vatican II's 1965 pastoral constitution on the Church in the modern world.

Laborem Exercens ("Performing Work")—Pope John Paul II's 1981 encyclical on human work on the ninetieth anniversary of *Rerum Novarum* ("On Capital and Labor").

Lumen Gentium ("The Light of Nations")—Vatican II's 1964 dogmatic constitution on the Church.

Ordinatio Sacerdotalis ("Priestly Ordination")—1994 apostolic letter of Pope John Paul II addressed to Catholic bishops, on reserving priestly ordination to men alone.

Pacem in Terris ("Peace on Earth")—1963 encyclical letter of Pope John XXIII on establishing universal peace in truth, justice, charity, and liberty.

Pornography and Violence in the Communications Media: A Pastoral Response—1989 document from the Pontifical Office for Social Communications.

Redemptor Hominis ("The Redeemer of the Human Person") —1979 encyclical of Pope John Paul II on redemption and the dignity of the human race.

Redemptoris Missio ("The Mission of the Redeemer")—Pope John Paul II's 1990 encyclical on the permanent validity of the Church's missionary mandate.

Sacrosanctum Concilium ("The Sacred Council")—Vatican II's 1963 constitution on the sacred liturgy.

Sacrum Diaconatus Ordinem ("The Sacred Order of the Deaconate")—Pope Paul VI's 1967 apostolic letter restoring the deaconate in the Latin Church.